Jesus Christ
Defeating Demons and Setting Captives Free

Reports from the Frontlines of an
Outpouring of the Holy Spirit

Zeb Bradford Long

DEDICATION

To the coworkers at the Presbyterian Bible College and Presbyterian Lay Training Center in Hsien Chu, Taiwan between 1982-1989 who took part in this great move of the Holy Spirit advancing the Kingdom of Jesus Christ.
And to those who experienced firsthand the power of the Devil, but even more the love and grace and freedom of Jesus Christ.

The painting on the cover "The Descent of the Dove" was done by Peggy Bradford Long, my mother, who taught me that with the outpouring of the Holy Spirit, Jesus Christ is manifested and demons are cast out as the Kingdom of God is advanced.

"But if I cast out demons by the Spirit of God, then the kingdom of God has already overtaken you."
Matthew 12:28 NET

CONTENTS

ACKNOWLEDGMENTS

I acknowledge with thanksgiving my teachers in deliverance ministry, the Rev. Archer Torrey and the Rev. Tom White, who walked ahead of me and with me in preparing the way for a mighty outpouring of the Holy Spirit that took place in Taiwan from 1980 through 1989.

I am most grateful for the support group of missionaries who provided the spiritual friendship and wise council that upheld Laura and me during this time of extraordinary blessing, but also of intense spiritual warfare. From the Presbyterian Church of Canada were Grace and Clare McGill, and Ted and Marylin Ellis. From the Presbyterian Church (USA) were Don and Virginia McCall and Lucy and Paul Alexander. Above all, as friends and coworkers as well as accountability partners, were Canadian missionaries Paul and Marybeth McClean and Ken Shay of Operation Mobilization.

I must also thank the President of the Presbyterian Bible College, the Rev. Earnest Wang, who welcomed me as a visionary and leader to the Bible College, first as Academic Dean and then as Vice-President.

I am grateful for the team of faculty and staff members of the Bible College who prepared the way for the outpouring of the Holy Spirit that took place at the College. They were the core prayer group, the vanguard of the prayer team that supported our role in this work. These were Rev. Timothy Whang, Rev. and Mrs. Lu, Miss Grace Chen, and Miss Charity Chen. We all grew together as a team.

I could have done none of this work in Taiwan as a young missionary from America without the full support and wise oversight of three leaders in the Taiwan Presbyterian Church: Acting General Secretary of the GA, the Rev. Andrew Hsieh; and after being released from prison, the General Secretary of the TPC, the Rev. Gau.

A special word of thanks to Elder Howard Chow of Suang-Lien Presbyterian Church in Taipei who shared with me the vision of not just the renewal of the Church in Taiwan, but of reaching Japan and China with the Gospel of Jesus Christ. He was instrumental in having the spiritual, relational, and financial resources to undertake this work in Taiwan, but also of opening doors in China and in Japan as well in building the Community of the Cross in the USA.

Above all I offer my thanks to my wife Laura who walked with me through this exciting and difficult time of raising a family and starting and running the English Department at the Bible College while living with me in this cross-cultural revival context. Whatever affirmation I may have received from being publicly in leadership—and I received a lot!—she deserves much more, for the often lonely and difficult behind the scenes role that she played in this amazing period of our lives together. I would not have able to cooperate with the Holy Spirit during this period without her love and support.

1

THE OUTPOURING OF THE HOLY SPIRIT IN TAIWAN

This book is a highly personal account of encounters with evil spirits that took place during my term of service as a Presbyterian Missionary in Taiwan.

My purpose in this book is to present in some detail the encounters with the demonic that took place while serving as a Presbyterian Missionary in Taiwan from the years 1980-1989. Most of the experiences to be described occurred from 1987-1989. This was a period of an outpouring of the Holy Spirit advancing the Kingdom of God by bringing revival among Presbyterians and other denominations. During this period, the preaching of the Gospel was often accompanied by signs and wonders.

This is a subject that I find difficult to talk about off the mission field and out of the unique context of an extraordinary movement of the Holy Spirit. This is first of all because most Western Christians have a worldview that discounts the present day reality of demons. So the moment one starts to talk about such things one risks not only being misunderstood, but also being consigned to the category of religious fanatic or worse. A second reason I hesitate to talk about this is because our focus should not be upon evil spirits but upon Christ. There is the very real danger of becoming so fascinated with the darkness that we are led into it.

As dangerous as this area is, we must still face it. The biblical worldview clearly includes demons. Further, setting people free from evil spirits was an essential part of Christ's work while He was in the flesh. He continues to this day the same work through the Holy Spirit. Thus, if we are to effectively minister in His name, we must face this awful subject and prepare ourselves to deal with it.

A great privilege that one has when called to the foreign mission field, especially during times of revival, is that one may experience things that are outside one's "normal" sphere of experienced reality. I often heard volunteer missionary doctors say that in their short visits to Taiwan they were privileged to have treated a greater variety and more advanced conditions than they had met in all their previous practice. I feel the same way! These experiences from within another culture, by their very extremity, may provide glimpses into aspects of objective reality that have been relegated to the fringes of our experience and consciousness by our Western worldview.

This period of my missionary service in Taiwan was also unique because it was a time of an outpouring of the Holy Spirit. The Kingdom of God was being powerfully advanced through the preaching of the Gospel accompanied by signs and wonders.

All though the history of the Church, such periods of the grace of Jesus Christ being manifested through signs and wonders are also accompanied by an intensification of spiritual warfare and manifestations of evil spirits. This is what we saw in Jesus' own ministry. Wherever He went, there were extraordinary evidences of the presence of the Kingdom of God. The people were amazed because unlike their experts on the law, He preached with authority. (Matthew 7:28-29) Power went forth from Jesus to heal so everyone wanted to touch Him. (Luke 6:19) Through Jesus the mighty power of God was expressed so that demons manifested their presence and were driven out of people. (Luke 9:43) With all these astonishing expressions both of the presence of God as well as of Satan, it is little wonder that many people were overwhelmed and at times confused. Some even thought that Jesus was casting demons out by the power of the ruler of demons, Beelzebub. (Luke 11:15) But Jesus corrected this misimpression by telling the true astonishing significance of the signs and wonders and the manifestations of evil. "But if I cast out demons by the Spirit of God, then the kingdom of God has already overtaken you." (Matthew 12:28)

I experienced Jesus doing all of this during the period of Kingdom advancement in Taiwan.

The experiences that follow are not offered as scientific proof of the reality of evil spirits. Rather they are experiences that persuaded me of their existence, and deepened my faith in the sovereignty, love, and power of Jesus Christ.

Though I bring certain theological presuppositions to this book, this is not theological reflection on the nature of evil or the demonic, rather it is personal testimony to the reality of evil spirits and to the greater reality of Jesus Christ. It is also a tribute to courageous individuals who dared to fight the darkness through the blood of Jesus.

2

PREPARATION FOR THE BATTLE

A ministry of healing of those who are afflicted by evil spirits is not something that I sought out or even desired. Rather, the more the Holy Spirit has worked to bring the Kingdom of God, the more we have been forced to deal with the demonic. As the Kingdom of Christ is manifested in power and in love, the powers of Satan are exposed and overcome. We have entered deliverance ministry by obediently proclaiming Jesus Christ, and following what the Holy Spirit was doing.

I was led into this ministry also by compassion. When I minister to people who are oppressed by Satan, usually through no fault of their own, it stirs up in me a holy war attitude. I want to see these people set free and healed for their own sakes and for the advancement of Christ's Kingdom.

As preparation for the work in Taiwan, my worldview had to undergo a shift. Without abandoning a healthy Western scientific skepticism, it came to include an appreciation for the spiritual and the supernatural.

From my early childhood I was predisposed to take seriously the spiritual realm. My mother was a vibrant Christian and great believer in prayer. In addition to the Bible, she brought me up on the writings of C. S. Lewis and George McDonald. Both of these authors presuppose a worldview in which there is an intermingling of the visible world with the invisible.

ENCOUNTERS WITH THE DEMONIC SPIRITS AT COLLEGE

During my years 1970-1974 as a student at Davidson College, a Presbyterian liberal arts college in the southern United States, I was exposed to the occult as it was associated with the drug culture. Being a Christian I did not get personally involved, but I witnessed some of the effects upon other students.

For instance, one of the coeds was very much sought after as a reader of tarot cards. She and others also had séances, all for fun of course, in their dorm rooms. One night she came bursting into my room—hair and clothes disheveled and with terror in her eyes. She frantically told me that while walking across campus something invisible had attacked her by tearing at her clothes and throat. She begged me to pray that it would go away. Having no experience with this sort of thing, I stammered out an awkward prayer in the name of Jesus. Immediately she was at peace. I warned her that even worse things were ahead if she did not stop meddling in the occult.

Another time I had a direct terrifying encounter with some type of high level demon that shook my worldview to the core. It happened one December evening. A girlfriend and I were driving back to campus from a Christmas concert in a nearby city. I was a committed Christian, although my girlfriend was not.

It was a cold, clear, brilliant moonlit night. Rather than go straight back to our dormitories, since the night was still young, we pulled off the main road onto a dirt road that ran through an empty field. The moment we did, I felt a cold chill run through me as I became distinctly aware of an evil presence nearby.

"Do you feel anything?" I asked.

"Yes," she replied in a shaky voice. "What is it?"

A force or power was instilling terror in me that made me want to run, but at the same time it was strangely drawing me.

"I don't know," I replied. "But why don't we go see what it is?"

It seems incredible that I would have suggested such a foolish thing! But we both got out of the car and walked slowly down the road. My girlfriend was clinging to me. The full moon was so bright that we had no need of a flashlight. All details were brilliantly clear.

As we walked, the force got stronger. I had not yet been given the gift of tongues, so I simply prayed over and over, "Lord Jesus, protect us. Lord Jesus, protect us."

I knew we were in the presence of something radically evil. I also knew deep inside that I was safe in Christ.

Suddenly we both looked off to the [left] side of the road. There in the field, not more than fifty feet away, was a black shape.

Language fails me when I attempt to describe exactly what we saw. It was much bigger than a man, yet at the same time seemed concentrated in a single point. It was black on black—a blackness that sucked up and annihilated reality. It almost seemed that we were looking into a void of non-created nothingness. The surging power emanating from this shape both repelled and attracted me. It was the sort of attraction to annihilation that one sometimes gets while looking off a high place and feeling the compelling urge to jump.

We stopped in our tracks and, without saying a word, started to back up step by step and retreat to the car. I dared not turn and run for fear it would leap onto my back and consume me. All the while I prayed, while my girlfriend clung desperately to me for protection.

No sooner had we taken a few steps backward than the thing began silently and slowly to glide toward us. With this the girl lost all control. She started screaming frantically and bolted to the car.

Something within me held firm. I retreated slowly, all the while praying and holding up my hands in command, as if to fend it off. Soundlessly the thing advanced on me, but it did not get much closer. Finally I got to the car, tore out of the place and headed back to the school as fast as I could drive.

We could see nothing now, but we could still feel the awful presence pursuing us and threatening to engulf us in its blackness. All the while my girlfriend screamed hysterically and struggled to throw herself out the window. I drove with one hand and constrained her with the other.

When we arrived at the campus, I drove right over the grass to the door of the small college chapel. Jumping out, I dragged the girl behind me and ran to the altar, where we both fell down in front of the cross.

"We belong to Jesus Christ," I shouted, "and not to your darkness! In the name of Jesus Christ, be gone!"

Suddenly it was gone. Everything snapped back to normal. We were no longer about to be sucked into nonexistence.

Later, astonishingly, my girlfriend could remember nothing of this experience.

This incident altered my view of reality profoundly. I think God let me confront Satan so I would know his existence experientially. There was also some refining going on. This experience of Satan may have been invited by the sinful possibilities inherent in my relationship with my girlfriend. The encounter with radical evil laid bare our souls, enabling me to see that my girlfriend was not a suitable companion for me to share my life of following Jesus Christ. The encounter also revealed my own sinful nature, which had been horribly fascinated by and actually attracted to this raw power of evil.

Actually several years later I encountered this same evil presence. This time with Laura Cole. We were engaged to be married. It was also a cold December night. We were sitting in the car waiting, praying together before going in to meet the Presbytery to begin the process of ordination.

Suddenly, just as in the field, I felt the same life-annihilating evil presence near the car. I turned to Laura and said, "Do you feel that?"

"Yes!" she shouted joyfully. "Praise God! Hallelujah! We belong to Jesus Christ, who is the victor!"

Instantly the evil presence departed.

That night the Lord sealed in my heart a certainty that Laura was the helpmate who was to walk with me into the spiritual adventures ahead. I also knew once again that Satan was real, but that Jesus Christ was even more real, and that He had defeated Satan on the Cross.

This and other such experiences worked toward expanding my worldview. The real change came, however, after both Laura and I had been baptized with the Holy Spirit in 1976 while we were serving as short-term missionaries in Korea for the Presbyterian Church in the United States. After praying and being baptized with the Holy Spirit, our eyes seemed to be opened to spiritual realities as never before. We also started to experience the gifts of the Holy Spirit as we were learning to cooperate with Jesus Christ in ministry.

A MIDNIGHT ATTACK BY A HOST OF EVIL SPIRITS IN KOREA

One experience which followed shortly after receiving the Baptism in the Holy Spirit stands out as a clear encounter with the demonic. This experience profoundly altered my concept of reality and greatly strengthened my faith in the power of Jesus Christ. I relate it below:

The year in Korea was very difficult. We had very poor living conditions, and found daily living an arduous test of patience.

Providentially for us, some wealthy friends of my family also lived in Seoul. They lived in a well-furnished, big, western style house with lots of servants. Occasionally we would flee to their home for a good meal, hot baths, television, and the other comforts of western culture. We always enjoyed these times, but there was something about their home that made us slightly uncomfortable. Time and space there had an oppressive heavy quality about it that eluded clear definition. There was also something vaguely odd about one of the Korean housekeepers. We were aware that the couple was also having severe marital problems.

On one such visit I stayed up late talking to the missus. She started telling me about how she would most likely be getting a divorce. She said again and again that her husband just did not love her—a statement that puzzled me for it was outwardly obvious that he did love her. After listening a long time, we had a prayer. During the prayer a wild thought came into my head, "the person she wants the divorce from is her father not her husband." Very tentatively I asked her what her relationship with her father was like. "Oh! He's been dead ten years," she said, then she fell silent. When I looked up tears were streaming down her face. Between sobs she told of how she had been rejected and unloved by her father.

At last I asked whether she might be able to forgive her father. As we prayed, she did. With a look of peace on her face that I had not seen the whole time we had known them in Korea, she went off to her bedroom and I to mine. It was about one in the morning. I was wide awake but decided to go to bed anyway.

In our bedroom, I found that Laura was still awake. She said something just did not feel right. I went to bed and Laura got up to go to the bathroom. When she returned she said, "Brad, there is something in this house that hates us." When she said this I felt it too. There seemed to be a malignant presence in the room. We decided that we should just pray right then and there against whatever it was. The door was shut, the lights were on, and we sat on the edge of the bed wrapped in the covers against the cold and started praying. We asked for protection, but not knowing really how to pray we prayed mostly in tongues. We asked the Holy Spirit to guide us and give us the names of any evil things that may be there.

As we prayed we tried various names but none of them fit. Suddenly, we were under attack! Something invisible, but extremely hostile, which felt like a black unclean wave, swept over us. With it there came to both of us at the same time, the Korean housekeeper's name. We both called out the name, and in the name of Jesus commanded it to leave. What happened for the next twenty minutes or so is impossible to describe. I have no clear language to describe these invisible, yet perceptible adversaries that were attacking us.

We found ourselves engaged in an intense struggle with one group of spirits after another. Names would come to us like lust, materialism, greed, envy, etc. Each time we felt them coming at us like blasts of foul smelling, dirty air, we would proclaim the name of Jesus and command them to leave. By this time we were both standing up on the bed praying in tongues at the top of our voices.

At one point there was a lull in the attacks, but the room was so swirling with presences and charged with evil power that we were afraid that things would literally start flying around. So we left the seeming safe fortress of our bed and removed all the pictures, vases and other objects from the dressers and walls and put them on the floor. Then came another series of attacks, but without the intensity of the first. Whenever there would be a lull, we would pray in the name of Jesus that if there were any others, they would be exposed.

During one of the lulls, at the strong prompting of the Holy Spirit, while carrying my cross, I walked through every room in the house except the couple's bedroom, and declared the name of Jesus in them and prayed for cleansing.

At last, after about an hour of this, there were no more attacks. Then Laura had a vision of a strong angel carrying a sword marching back and forth through the house. Then, exhausted, we went peacefully to sleep.

Whether the couple heard anything or not we do not know. To this day they have never said anything, and we were afraid to ask.

After this strange midnight foray into the supernatural, there was a subtle but definite change in the atmosphere of the home. The heaviness was lifted. The couple also seemed more settled, and they did not get a divorce.

For weeks after this I felt unclean. I mentioned this to several Presbyterian missionaries, but received no help. Finally at a conference I was talking to a Catholic priest about the whole experience. When I mentioned that I felt unclean, he said, in a most matter of fact way, "Sure. Every time I cast out demons I feel unclean too!" So we prayed right there and I felt cleansed.

This experience profoundly shaped my worldview. We knew that, though often hidden in the fabric of human sinfulness, the demonic was real. At the same time, we experientially knew that the powers of Satan had been overcome by Jesus Christ.

After this awakening I continued to grow in awareness of spiritual warfare. Another very important learning time was my wilderness experience of serving a strife-torn church in North Carolina for two years. During this period I vividly encountered the demonic in the church and in my own life. This, however, was not a time of deliverance ministry. That was to await the outpouring of the Holy Spirit which was to take place in Taiwan.

MY TEACHERS IN THIS AREA OF DELIVERANCE MINISTRY

My first teacher was an Episcopal missionary to Korea, Father Archer Torrey, founder of Jesus Abbey. He taught clearly on this esoteric subject. Ministering with him in healing and deliverance also provided many opportunities for practical learning.

In August 1988 a team headed by Dr. Charles Kraft of Fuller Theological Seminary came to Taiwan. On the team was a conservative Baptist Pastor named Tom White of Front Line Ministries from Oregon. Tom's specialty is spiritual warfare and deliverance. During this time I took part in the deliverance of a dear friend and co-worker who had been demonized since her traumatic childhood. Through this and other experiences of ministering with Tom, my gifts of discernment were sharpened. From him I also learned practical ways of dealing with evil spirits.

Tom, above all, helped me learn how to see. As I followed him around in ministry serving as his translator, he would often say, "Look, did you see that one; it's right around the eyes. Or there! That demon is manifesting through tension on the left temple." I did not see a thing! But then one evening as we ministered to a young man, my awareness began to change. Tom, while looking straight at the young man, commanded the evil spirit to manifest. Then turning to me in English said, "Quick! Look! There! In the eyes. Do you see the spirit?" No, I really did not. And though I was feeling rather stupid about being so blind, I said so. As the deliverance prayer proceeded, all the time I translated I kept looking into the man's eyes trying to figure out what Tom was seeing that I missed. Then Tom commanded the spirit to leave. Suddenly I saw it. There was a momentary, elusive something passing over the man's eyes, like a shadow. From then on I seemed to be able to see better because I knew what sort of subtle evidences to look for. The seeing was both an actual physical seeing as well as an inward spiritual awareness.

Late one night, after dealing with some of my own needs for confession and emotional healing, Tom White prayed for Ken Shay and me. He prayed that we would be anointed to set others free from the power of evil spirits, and be equipped to lead in strategic spiritual warfare. From that time on I have found myself empowered for this ministry. At the same time in Taiwan, I found myself surrounded by a team of loving, supportive, Spirit-anointed co-workers.

I must stress, for the sake of balance, that even though this book focuses on the demonic, this was not the primary thrust of our mission work. Our passion was for helping the Taiwanese to know and to experience Jesus Christ. We also worked to disciple others which included leading people into receiving and operating in the gifts of the Holy Spirit for the upbuilding and expansion of the Church. In Taiwan I was Vice-Principal of the Presbyterian Bible College, and Director of the Presbyterian Lay Training Center. I was not an exorcist! I was an educator and an evangelist! But as I did evangelistic missions, moving in the power of the Holy Spirit in preaching and healing ministry, I found myself continually engaged with evil spirits.

3

TEAM MINISTRY FOR DELIVERANCE

The Lay Training Center was established in 1982 at the Presbyterian Bible College in Hsinchu, Taiwan. The Center provided the context in which I developed retreats and conferences that introduced the work of the Holy Spirit and helped Christians grow in power ministry. We started off very small, but by 1988 great momentum had built up, with many doors opening for ministry throughout the island. At this point, signs and wonders started to be a normal part of the movement. We also found ourselves constantly dealing with the demonic.

These manifestations of signs and wonders correlated with the maturation of a prayer group into a power ministry team. This team consisted of five formal members—all, with one exception, co-workers at the Lay Training Center. In addition, there was a large circle of around twenty other team members who supported in active prayer and participated in the actual deliverance sessions when they are able to. This Holy Spirit-anointed team displayed a great diversity of gifts. They were also willing to share leadership and to allow a full expression of everyone's gifts.

Much of the leadership fell to me, but it was very fluid as we all took part, and as different gifts were required. My role was often like that of a coordinator to keep us all working together in flow with the Holy Spirit. Many times when I have been dealing with a case or leading a prayer meeting, others have been anointed to act as coordinators. I encouraged others to move into leadership as soon as they were equipped to do so.

The team worked corporately and individually to maintain our own life of prayer and to learn as much about the subject as possible. Among the extended support group, most had been through the conferences and training programs offered at the Lay Training Center from 1982 until 1987. Of great help to me personally was the power encounter study group led by Ken Shay. This group consisted of other missionaries engaged in ministry. We met regularly for prayer and to reflect on what the Holy Spirit was doing. We were also led by Ken in systematic biblical and theological study of power encounter topics.

THE MINISTRY TEAM MEMBERS

To give some flavor of the diversity of people involved and the way that we functioned as a team, here is an introduction to some of the key people:

1. Rev. Don Decker—a retired Presbyterian minister with certification in counseling. He tended to see things in terms of psychology and was very adept at diagnosing emotional and psychological problems. Don maintained a healthy skepticism regarding the reality of demons. He tended to see them in terms

of autonomous psychological complexes and regarded the prayers for deliverance as an extreme but highly effective form of therapy. Don is a man of mature faith and deep compassion for those who suffer. He also had DSM–3 in his head and was very apt at identifying mental illness and other psychological problems.

2. Rev. George Shu—a co-worker at the Lay Training Center since July, 1988. He has a sharp, analytical mind that seeks to clearly and systematically understand everything that is going on from a theological and sociological point of view. He brought an extensive knowledge of Chinese culture and the classics.

3. Jean Shu—George's wife who has undergone deliverance and so understands some of the dynamics of oppression from personal experience. She is gifted in leading anointed praise and worship. She is deeply sensitive to the hurts of others and is developing a ministry of healing.

4. Rev. Ken Shay—an Overseas Crusade missionary. Ken studied at Fuller Theological Seminary and has had a long-term interest in the area of power encounter. During nine years of missionary service in Taiwan, he did extensive research in this area. He moves freely in the gifts of the Holy Spirit. Because he is also a weight-lifter, he often found himself in the role of restraining people. He was also a great personal friend and to me a brother in Christ.

5. Mr. Howard Dezo—the Assistant Director of the Lay Training Center. Howard is a Christian businessman who loves the Lord and loves others. He moves freely in the gifts of the Holy Spirit, and when he prayed for people they would often "go down under the power of the Spirit." His gift is a great zeal for the Lord, and a great love for people.

There were around twenty other team members from different backgrounds and levels of experience.

Among this extended team three persons deserve special mention. The Rev. and Mrs. Peng, former pastor of Suang-Lien Presbyterian Church in Taipei. This couple attended nearly every event sponsored by the Lay Training Center. After Dr. Kraft led a power ministry conference in August of 1988, Rev. Peng welcomed us to conduct a monthly prayer meeting at Suang-Lien Church. The purpose of this meeting was to provide the opportunity for Presbyterians in Taipei to experience the power ministry. Reverend Peng and I would often share in the teaching and leading of these meetings. The Pengs often worked as an effective team in praying for deliverance.

Timothy Huang was the first faculty member of the College to be filled with the Holy Spirit while on a trip to Jesus Abbey in Korea. He was a steadfast friend during this entire period. Charity Chen was the first student filled with the Holy Spirit while at a Prayer Mountain. Later she went through inner healing and deliverance and became an important member of the team, a role she continued in after enrolling at Tainan Seminary. Charity was gifted in healing prayer and prophetic ministry.

Another person who played a vital role in this ministry was Miss Grace Lwo, a student at Taiwan Theological Seminary. Prior to enrolling at the seminary, she had served as my assistant at the Lay Training Center, developing the power ministry program and teaching materials. She freely moved in the gifts of the Spirit, and was especially gifted in discernment.

Among the team members, all of the manifestational gifts of the Holy Spirit as listed in I Cor. 12,14 were evidenced. This is not to imply that all of these people were present at each deliverance session. Usually it was four to six.

In addition to these there were others who did not often take part in the events, but served as intercessors from the small prayer group at the Bible college. Among them were Mrs. Colene Lu and Mr. Lu and Miss Rosemary Yuan, all professors at the college.

Above all, there was Laura, my wife, who provided invaluable support during this period of intensive ministry. Without the covering and protection provided by her and our home, it would have been impossible for me to venture out into ministry.

I list all these people to demonstrate that though I was often the "point man"; I was not in this alone. Nor was the healing power from me. Rather healing of the demonized took place through the Body of Jesus Christ.

FRUIT FOR THE KINGDOM OF GOD

My family, including our young children Elizabeth, Rebecca, and Stephen, were also involved and impacted by this amazing time of the movement of the Holy Spirit. We experienced spiritual warfare and some sustained demonic attacks. The Lord, however, did shower us with blessings and produced fruit for the Kingdom.

Once we had a very proper unchurched English family over for tea. Their daughter was a friend with our eight-year-old Elizabeth. In the middle of tea time, there came an urgent knock on the door. I jumped up and was followed by Elizabeth to the door. A group of terrified students in Chinese said, "It is a really big demon and we can't get it out. Please help!" My daughter who was fluent in Chinese asked if she could come too to fight the demon. I said no she needed to stay with her friend.

When I got back, Elizabeth, jumped up and said, "Daddy did you cast them out?" The English couple asked, "What? Do you have rats?" "Oh no! We have demons! Don't you know that my daddy is a ghostbuster!" Their response was "Oh my! Is that stuff real?" God used this incident to lead them to faith. They became faithful members of our home church group.

These demonstrations of the power of Jesus over the Devil had many often surprising and unexpected results for the Kingdom of God.

4

OCCASIONS FOR ENCOUNTERS WITH DEMONS

Most of the deliverance cases that we dealt with just happened as we were leading prayer or evangelistic meetings. As we would move into times of anointed praise, or were laying on hands for healing or blessing, the demons would spontaneously begin to manifest. This is apparently what happened to Jesus when he spoke in the synagogue. A man with a demon started shouting "Ah!, What have you to do with us, Jesus of Nazareth? Have you come to destroy us?..." Jesus commanded him to be silent and to come out of the man. (Luke 4:31-36)

When this happened, there was usually no time for preparation or clear teaching. We were just thrust into spiritual battle. In severe cases the exorcism would continue long after the meeting had been concluded. Often there would be follow-up with further prayer and counseling.

For instance, once I was preaching at the Maundy Thursday Service at the Presbyterian Bible College. It was a two-hour noon worship service after which classes were to resume. As I was preaching on the crucifixion of Jesus, I felt in myself that the Holy Spirit was beginning to move in a powerful way. This was confirmed through empirical evidence such as tears and a stirring in the congregation. Suddenly, a young woman on one side of the chapel fell to the floor shrieking, "No Jesus! I don't want you! No! No!" Simultaneously, on the other side of the chapel a young man started acting strangely, making bizarre contortions. Nothing like this had ever happened before at a school service. What followed was remarkable! Classes did not resume. Instead the entire student body (about 120) and most of the faculty remained in the chapel in urgent prayer for the rest of the day and on into the evening. Not only were the two students dramatically delivered from evil spirits, but also many students accepted Jesus Christ, and most of those who were already Christians experienced the baptism with the Holy Spirit.

Another context for dealing with evil spirits was during prayers for emotional healing. This often took place on intensive retreats and in one-on-one counseling sessions rather than in public meetings.

As word of what God was doing spread, ministers started bringing to us persons whom they believed were demonized. Most of these cases, however, proved not to be evil spirits but mental illness. These I referred to professionals for counseling, therapy or hospitalization.

It must be affirmed that in most places where these manifestations occurred, there had been no previous conditioning to shape the behaviors that we observed. Often we ministered in Taiwan Presbyterian Churches in which there is about as much openness and experience of the demonic as there is in the average Presbyterian Church in America; which is to say very little. Also, in our revival meetings we generally did not teach on the demonic nor tell stories of deliverance. Our focus was on proclaiming Jesus Christ as the way of salvation.

FIVE TYPES OF DEMONIC EXPERIENCE

Each case that I dealt with in Taiwan was a different and unique learning experience. Despite this diversity, these experiences fell naturally into five general categories. These are as follows:

1. External demonic attack

2. Simple demonic oppression

3. Complex demonic oppression related to inner hurts and/or occult activity

4. A person used as a staging area for demonic attack against a church, ministry, or nation

5. Strategic spiritual warfare as preparation for Kingdom advance

The following chapters give detailed descriptions of each type with examples. These selected examples are actual cases, but names and circumstances have been altered to rule out any possibility of identification. One exception is Charity Chen who has granted permission for her name to be included.

It will be noted that the most serious cases given are women. We did minister to many men. But in my limited experience, the majority of the more serious cases were women. I suspect that there are several reasons for this.

First, demonization is a form of victimization that follows human victimization. The place of women in Asia has been one that placed them at greater risk of sexual and physical abuse.

Second, in that culture, women seemed to be more free or more driven than men to seek help. This was evidenced in the fact that at the prayer or worship services there were usually more women than men present. However, we saw Jesus pour out His love and grace upon all who reached out to Him, regardless of gender or station in life or even whether they were believers or not.

5

TYPE ONE: EXTERNAL DEMONIC ATTACK

In this case there is a sudden demonic assault made upon a person from without. It may come as outward circumstances or from one's own mind and emotions. It is meant to hinder the person's effectiveness in the Kingdom of God. The spirit does not seem to attach itself to the person nor enter into the person. If, however, these attacks are not resisted, they may become the occasion for further demonic control. It may be this type of attack that Paul refers to in Ephesians 6:16 as "flaming darts of the evil one."

1. Attacks that come as temptations through our thoughts or through circumstances

These flaming darts may come as an intense temptation that comes from outside the person, but resonate with an inner weakness, urge, or desire. For instance, the person prone to excessive drinking may find himself in circumstances where he is offered a drink. The attack may also come as thoughts that almost possess us and urge us to some action that is destructive to ourselves or to others. For instance, while standing in a high place, a person hears or has the sudden impulse to "Jump, just jump." Sometimes these darts come as bouts of irrational discouragement or despair.

Such flaming darts would often hit me while on the way to a meeting where power ministry would take place. For this reason I made it a rule to always be accompanied by other praying team members. Once, however, I had to travel to a healing meeting alone. On the way I had to pass several barber shops. Many barber shops in Taiwan are notorious for offering services far beyond just cutting hair. As I drove by, scarcely noticing these places—for they are just about everywhere—I was suddenly seized by a wild irrational lust. I seemed in the grip of some supernatural force that would draw me into one of the shops. It was by strong resolution of will and constant calling upon the name of Jesus that I made it to the meeting. I immediately asked the team to pray for me, and the obsession left as quickly as it had come.

One must be careful not to identify all such temptations as coming from demons. Without doubt, most arise from our fallen sinful nature that still persists within us even though we are in Jesus Christ.

The Devil is clever; he does not play fair. As the Holy Spirit worked with increasing effectiveness at the renewal events, the attacks against our families seemed to intensify. Usually the day before leaving was incredibly difficult with lots of irrational hassles and tensions. Then while at the meeting, those at home often came under attack.

Once while I was at an important meeting in Taipei, very much in power ministry, Laura was at home waiting up for me. As she waited she became vaguely aware of the presence of evil in the house. As time passed she became aware that something dark was closing in around her. She considered calling her friend Marybeth, a Canadian missionary. But since the hour was late and nothing tangible was happening, she was hesitant to call. This unease and awareness of being under attack continued to grow in intensity until at around 11:00 o'clock, it suddenly lifted.

A few days later, we shared with Marybeth what had happened. With great surprise she said, "Why the Lord was looking after you! On that very night at around 11:00 I had the strongest feeling that something was wrong and that Paul and I had to pray for Laura. As we prayed asking for guidance, I had a mental image of a terrible-looking old hag shaped thing gliding toward your house. As we prayed in the name of Jesus, it turned away and disappeared into the bamboo patch beside your house. I almost called, but since it was around 11:00 pm I did not want to wake you up. I was also afraid it was all just my imagination."

Usually such attacks were vague and confusing, but the resulting fear, tensions, communication breakdowns, and temptations were very real.

2. Attacks that comes as a physical assault against us

At other times an external demonic attack may come as a physical assault. Once I was driving to a large healing meeting in Taipei where I was to be the keynote speaker. Suddenly, in the car I felt a dark power or force assault me. I knew its intention was to kill me. At that same moment a large truck swerved wildly in front of me. I was barely saved from a collision by quick reflexes. In the moment just before this occurred, before I was aware of what was happening, I was suddenly moved to pray in tongues. This was surely the Holy Spirit praying through me to resist the devil. I promptly returned home and took the train!

Another form of physical attack comes at night. Many people have reported that they awake from sleep (or even before going to sleep) to find a horrible black presence pressing down upon them, choking or suffocating them. They fight against the presence, but find themselves powerless. They try to scream for help, but cannot speak. Usually it is by calling on the name of Jesus Christ, in thought and then verbally, that the evil spirit leaves.

For several years at the Bible College, whoever was assigned to a particular room in the women's dorm would have these disturbing night experiences. After praying for the rooms, these disturbances ceased.

I have had one such experience. This took place not in Taiwan, but in the United States. After I took the job of Executive Director of PRRMI, we went through some periods of intensive spiritual warfare. During the height of this period, I awoke in the middle of the night in terror, suffocating with a black, heavy presence pressing down on my face. In the fast-fading images of a dream, I saw fragments of a hideous demonic face glaring at me. It seemed only with great struggle that I was able to first form in my mind, the words "Jesus help!" and then to say His name out loud. As I did the presence lifted, seemed to linger in the room for a few moments and then left. As I prayed in the Spirit, I felt as clearly as if spoken verbally the words, "Mobilize my people, for spiritual warfare." I do not doubt that that was Jesus speaking to me, giving some marching orders for PRRMI's ministry. It is in response to that command that I have taken the risk of preparing this book and have included spiritual warfare as part of the Dunamis Project.

These experiences are so common that I have sought a physical or psychological explanation for them. There are some similarities between these experiences and DSM III R diagnostic criteria for panic disorder. There is clearly a connection in the symptoms, but they fit the disorder only if they are "unexpected, i.e. did not occur immediately before or on exposure to a situation that almost always caused anxiety..." An evil spirit would be a cause that would elicit the natural response of anxiety.

3. Subtle but powerful temptations to misuse the Holy Spirit's power

The most potentially debilitating of all these "flaming dart" attacks are those that come while moving in empowered ministry. These attacks came in a diversity of forms. While in leadership I would experience barrages of doubts or irrational discouragement. Or there would be external distracting disturbances like the sound system going out or an evil spirit manifesting through someone and frightening a large group or disrupting crucial teaching or worship.

The most subtle and relentless, however, came in the form of the temptation to misuse or manipulate the Holy Spirit's power. Often this would come as the temptation to go beyond what God had actually said or was doing in order to fulfill the expectation of those who were present, and thus build oneself up in their eyes instead of giving all the glory to Jesus.

Once at a prayer meeting the Holy Spirit was moving, bringing some remarkable manifestations. Suddenly in my spirit I knew that the Lord was going to move in a powerful way, resting people in the Spirit. Since I had never been used in that way before, I was awkward about what to expect next. Then came a strong nudge to walk across the room and lay hands on the pastor. I thought, "Surely, Lord, you could start with someone a little easier!" Nonetheless I obeyed, and no sooner had I barely touched his forehead when I experienced a heady surge of power go through me and the man fell on the floor with a heavy thud. When the people saw their pastor go down, the atmosphere of the meeting became electric with the people's excitement, faith, and eager expectation. I immediately was aware through the inward nudging of the Holy Spirit as well as the people's expressions, that six others were also to receive this blessing. As I went from one to another, they all instantly went down with the slightest touch, lying on the floor abandoned to peace and joy. As each person went down I felt the Holy Spirit's power rushing through me. It was an invigorating, almost erotic sensation of pure power.

Suddenly, the power ceased and I felt the Holy Spirit saying, "That is all I am doing." The instant the Holy Spirit spoke, there arose another voice, which was the Tempter speaking in perfect harmony with my ego. "Look, the people are ready, just do a few more." I observed that many in the group were eagerly expectant that God would so bless them. The group psychology was all working in my favor and had accorded me great power of suggestion. I knew that all I had to do was to give them a little push and it would be received as the hand of God. I also knew that the people would think of me as a great Spirit-empowered missionary. But more than anything else, I found myself wanting that rush of power. There was a struggle within myself, but by the grace of God I was able to resist the Tempter. I invited everyone to kneel, offered up a prayer of thanks, and gave the benediction.

There is only one way to be in ministry empowered by the Holy Spirit. It is to obey in the same way that Jesus obeyed. "Truly, truly, the son does what he sees the father doing." (John 5:19)

The Tempter sought to get Jesus to use His power and authority on His own, and out of accord with the timing and intent of the Father. Once we, like Jesus, start to grow in the gifts and power of the Holy Spirit, we should be on guard, for we will be tempted in like manner.

The significant thing about all these occasions is that the attack is external, coming from outside the person. The demon does not attach itself to the person's body or psyche. Usually such attacks are transient, and are dealt with by putting on the armor of Christ and resisting the devil in the name of Jesus.

For me personally, I have found that to survive these attacks, especially the third form, it is essential to be in Christ-centered spiritual relationships that allow for vulnerability and regular confession.

Throughout the time of intensive power ministry in Taiwan, I met with a small group of other men who were involved in similar ministry. We would regularly reflect on what was happening to us spiritually. And we would hear one another's confessions.

Together, we sharpened the gifts of discernment. In a gentle, loving way we held one another accountable and protected one another through prayer.

6

TYPE TWO: SIMPLE DEMONIC OPPRESSION

There are other occasions, however, when a demon actually seems to attach itself to the person, but does not take deep root. It may find an opening through some sin such as anger, or by one being in a place where there are demons present. Usually, these may be dealt with by a simple command in the name of Jesus Christ. Often there is only one spirit and not a complex of them. Their departure may be signaled by a lifting perceived by the person and by those praying, or by some physical manifestation such as shaking or gagging. Frequently these manifestations are subtle and easily missed by the undiscerning eye. The following are examples of this type:

1. The student who was attacked while visiting a Buddhist temple

Once, when out doing evangelism in local temples, a group of us experienced a dark seductive power emanating from a temple. We prayed together and resisted it. But one of the other students, a pastor's daughter, arrived just after we left. She also experienced the same power, but was unable to resist, and found herself being drawn into the inner room of the temple. She described it later as a sense of dread, but also of irresistible fascination.

The inner room was filled with ornate ancient idols and hazy with incense smoke. In the center was an ancient dragon-inlaid box. The power emanated from the box.

Upon touching it, she felt an evil presence attach itself to her. For the next week she was tormented by nightmares, strange inner voices, and a sense of a blackness hovering around her. Though a very dedicated Christian, she was unable to pray or worship.

She came to me deeply distressed, fearing that she was going insane. With two other co-workers, I prayed for her, and in Mandarin Chinese started to command the spirit, in the name of Jesus, to leave. The spirit did not obey or give any response at all. The Holy Spirit suddenly seemed to speak to me saying, "This is an uneducated one; it does not understand Mandarin; use the local dialect." This is the language used by the people of the temple. I told my Chinese co-workers and they commanded it to leave in Taiwanese. It instantly obeyed. Its departure was evidenced by a sudden lifting in the girl's face, and by the sense of a black presence swirling through the room. There was no further trouble.

This student did very well in her studies and is presently in effective Christian ministry.

2. A spirit entering a pastor's wife through unforgiveness

At a retreat for Presbyterian pastors and their spouses, we entered an extended period of wonderful praise in the Spirit. During the full silence that followed, I received a word of knowledge revealing that God was going to heal someone with back trouble. I hoped it was me! My own back was really hurting. But one of the wives immediately stepped forward and asked for prayer. For a two-month period she had suffered from severe back pains. The pain was especially acute during Sunday worship. This person is well-balanced, spiritually mature, and often manifests gifts of the Holy Spirit.

As we laid our hands on her back while praying in tongues, she suddenly began to gag. I perceived that it was a demon and bound it in the name of Jesus. I then commanded it to reveal how it entered. Immediately she began to cry and said that two months ago she had been badly hurt by one of the families in the church, and had remained intensely angry. We led her in a prayer for forgiveness, and then commanded the spirit of anger to leave. With one violent spasm of retching it left. The back pain was instantly healed.

It was, I believe, the Christ-centered praise and the gift of knowledge that prepared the way for this person's deliverance.

3. The young man attacked by a spirit of lust

At a conference for college students, one of the small group leaders, an American, was brought to me for prayer. The young man was deeply discouraged about his inability to minister effectively to others. As I laid my hand upon his head, there flashed into my mind in big letters "LUST." I gently asked, "Would you also happen to be dealing with lust?" He looked up, surprised, and said, "Yes, that was the real problem." As we prayed we became aware that in addition to some natural weaknesses, a spirit of lust was there. When we commanded it to leave, there was a slight but visible change. His eyes flickered and a lightness infused his whole appearance. The young man returned to the meetings and found that though still attracted to several of the women in his group, he was no longer overwhelmed by lust. He found that he could minister effectively.

Attacks like this are relatively simple to deal with. The presence of the spirit is discerned, then commanded to leave. Usually it leaves without much struggle. Often the role that the oppressed person must play is to deal honestly with the reason why the spirit entered in. There is usually no need for extensive counseling and follow-up.

I have found that I can almost always deal with this type by myself or with one other team member. That is, if I am moving in the Holy Spirit. When I am not, I am unable to discern very clearly the existence of evil spirits, much less cast them out.

7

TYPE THREE: COMPLEX OPPRESSION RELATED TO EMOTIONAL HURTS AND OR OCCULT ACTIVITY

Some cases require an extended spiritual battle as well as emotional healing and extended counseling (and/or psychotherapy). Often in these cases there is a combination of deep emotional hurt, persistent sin, and occult involvement.

1. Relation to occult involvement

Most of the cases that I have dealt with in Taiwan have had some type of occult involvement. For some this has resulted from having been blessed by a spirit medium or offered to an idol at an early age by a parent or grandparent. For others it happened because the person has actively sought out a spirit medium or gone to a fortune teller. For many, they have worshiped the idols, either at home or in a temple. These types of activities, which are so clearly forbidden in scripture, really do open doors to the spiritual realm and bring the danger of bondage to evil spirits.

One may be tempted to assume that everyone who does these things will be bound by evil spirits. Certainly while outside of Christ, a person is in a form of spiritual bondage. But at conversion, most people are set free and cleansed. However, those who have had a history of deep hurt or persistent sin along with the occult activity often seem to need further deliverance ministry. For them, full freedom in Christ is often a struggle involving forgiveness, emotional healing, and casting out the evil spirit.

For the demons to leave who entered into the person because of the occult activity, there must be clear confession of sin and renunciation of the devil. When the person was offered up as a child by a parent or relative, they must break the soul-tie with that person.

Thus far, I have found it difficult to know whether the inner hurts made the person vulnerable to attack through the occult involvement, or whether the occult involvement opened the doors to the demons who then aggravated the emotional hurts.

2. A step-by-step process of emotional healing and deliverance

In all these cases, getting the person free from the spirits is an extended violent struggle. There often must be a step by step process alternating between counseling, prayer for emotional healing, and casting out the demons. In each of these cases there seems to have been whole constellations of demons attracted to the complexes of emotional hurts. As the demons leave, there is a great deal of retching and violent resistance. One also sees a great release of built-up emotion festering around the hurts.

Tears and intense expressions of anger, hatred, or hurt are common. Part of what seems to be expelled is the autonomous psychological complex.

This complex struggle can take many hours and several sessions. The deliverance sessions may also take place over many weeks or months apart before the job is finished. The prayer counseling and/or psychotherapy that must follow may also require many more sessions before there is complete healing. The deliverance is not a cure-all; rather, it is a way of removing some of the spiritual obstacles to healing.

3. The need for a process over time as the personality is restructured

This type of deliverance should be a process extended over time. As the demons are cast out and psychological complexes lose their centering power, a restructuring of the person's personality needs to happen. For instance, if deep hatred mixed with demonic infestation has provided the organizing energy for the person's personality; when this centering energy is removed, what will hold the personality together? If the deliverance takes place too quickly without the inner healing and re-structuring, the individual may have a complete personality breakdown resulting in suicide or mental illness.   In addition, during the deliverance the demons may be expected to counter-attack. So the person's faith and strength of personality must be slowly built up to withstand this counter-attack.

As the deliverance and emotional healing process take place, often there is the sense of going deeper and deeper. First, relatively simple or recent hurts are dealt with, and with them evil spirits. It seems the deeper one goes back in time, the more intensely the evil spirits are embedded. Often too, one may deal with many lesser spirits until finally getting to the more powerful controlling ones.

The following are examples of this type of complex oppression:

A. A young man possessed by a spirit urging him to become a Je Tung (a spirit medium)

A very strong young man was brought to me by his pastor. At a prayer meeting when he received the infilling with the Holy Spirit and began to speak in tongues, he became very violent and started to hit people. Then another personality seized him and began to speak through him in a strange trance-like manner.

In Taiwan, the spirit medium usually goes into a trance before the spirit begins to speak through him. In the mountain churches, however, one of the marks of the Spirit movement was of people falling into a trance and speaking words from the Holy Spirit. We decided that this was an evil spirit, not because of the trance (which may have been a cultural phenomenon) but because of the contents of the speaking and the man's lack of control. We could also tell from the fruits that this was not a spirit in accord with Jesus Christ.

The deliverance session lasted several hours and required a team of five people. We found a whole complex of personality and psychological problems arising from bad relationships with parents. In addition, there was considerable sexual sin. He was deeply involved in pornography, and had frequently been to prostitutes. He had also had many homosexual experiences, some of which were from a very early age when he had been abused by older men.

The occult connection was direct. His family was very much involved in a local temple. A brother-in-law had tried to get him to become a spirit medium. Apparently, even though the young man was a Christian, he had gone along with some of the spiritualist ceremonies.

The man confessed his occult activities as well as his other sins. A terrible struggle followed this as the spirits were bound and commanded to leave. He writhed about on the floor, tried to hit me, gagged and retched violently. At times he would go into a trance-like state and begin to speak in the way that a spirit medium does when possessed by a spirit. The spirit seemed to be speaking a mixture of Japanese and tribal dialect. The young man was Taiwanese and spoke neither of these other languages.

He left the session feeling much better. No longer did he have the strange manifestations when he started praying in tongues. He will, however, still need a great deal of emotional healing as well as counseling to overcome his other problems.

2. A case with no occult involvement but deep inner hurt

In other cases of this type, during or after a person has experienced spiritual gifts, demons manifest.

One such case was long and drawn out. When this person first came to me, I sensed that in addition to deep hurt and over control by her destructive mother, there was something demonic within her. This "feeling" of the demonic is hard to describe; it was as if there was something dark about her. Other people felt it too, and actually came privately to speak to me about it.

At my invitation and with her ready assent, we had several counseling sessions in which we found no occult involvement, only deep hurt. Unlike all the other cases, she came from a solid Presbyterian family. Both her parents were Presbyterian elders.

When I first prayed for her seeking discernment, there was no manifestation whatsoever. But I still sensed that there was something demonic entwined within her hurt and other psychological problems. In the prayer sessions that followed, we prayed for emotional healing, but made little progress. I suggested that she seek professional help, but this advice was rejected.

After four months of regularly attending a Charismatic prayer meeting, one evening she was wonderfully filled with the Holy Spirit. She prayed and sang in tongues and was overwhelmed with joy. Immediately, she had to lie down because of a terrible headache. She also started to gag. At this time I was unable to minister to her, but I knew that the demons were beginning to come to the surface.

A few weeks later, at another prayer meeting, she was again filled with the Holy Spirit and exhibited the same gagging behavior. I seized this opportunity to command the demons to manifest themselves. We engaged in a two-hour deliverance session in which many spirits were cast out. Things happened very quickly and with incredible intensity; it was as if things were bolting out of her as quickly as they were exposed. Despite the fact that we had bound them and commanded them not to hurt anyone, each group, as they left, seemed to viciously torment the poor girl with violent contortions and painful retching. It was horrible.

I know that some who teach on deliverance say that all you have to do is command the demon in the name of Jesus to be bound and not hurt anyone. Others say that you just tell them to come out peacefully without the gagging or screaming or other such obnoxious manifestations. Many times this is certainly true; at other times however, I have found that in dealing with demons of this high level who have such long standing grounds of entry, things are not so simple. Even when Jesus cast out demons, there were manifestations of the demon's malice. An instance is the story of the epileptic child. "...he rebuked the unclean spirit, saying to it, 'You dumb and deaf spirit, I command you, come out of him, and never enter him again.' And after crying out and convulsing him terribly, it came out, and the boy was like a corpse; so that most of them said, 'He is dead.'" (Mark 9:25-26.) This is an indication of the demons' malevolent, hateful nature. They thrive on pain and confusion.

For the next three or four prayer meetings as the Holy Spirit would start to move upon the group, the same thing would happen and more evil spirits would be cast out. Gradually the girl was freed from the black demonic oppression, but she is still afflicted with severe emotional problems that will require extensive counseling, love, and courage for healing. Now, however, with the demons gone, she is courageously facing the task ahead. She has willingly entered into therapy and is making slow but steady progress. Above all, she is growing in her relationship with Jesus Christ. She is gifted in leading worship, and is very effective in ministering to others who are in need of emotional healing.

3. The case of the woman with the fifteen demon faces

A very strange and moving case took place at a large Charismatic church. During a prayer meeting I was going from person to person praying that each would be filled with the Holy Spirit. I came to a petite woman about thirty years old. She had a sweet look on her face and was eager for me to pray for her. I placed my hand on her head and started to pray over her. The moment I spoke the name of Jesus, she fell down on the floor and started screaming in pain.

I was rather shaken, and at first was so confused that I did not know what to do. Thankfully, several of the women came and carried her screaming out of the room and I finished the prayer meeting. About thirty minutes later I found her still writhing and thrashing about. I commanded the spirits to settle down and not to hurt anyone. After a time they did; then I commanded them to tell us their name. The woman spoke these words, "I just am." Then she would make a grotesque distorted face. She could distort her face in the most horrible ways that seemed beyond human ability. She did this about fifteen times each time saying, "I just am." We were completely baffled as to what was going on until suddenly one of the Chinese ministry team members said, "Why those are the faces of those demons in Hell Temple tormenting the damned." In many Buddhist temples in Taiwan there are vivid paintings depicting the demons and the torments of hell. Rather than giving us their names, the afflicting spirits were showing us their awful faces.

After about an hour we got the woman settled down enough to do some talking. She was a Presbyterian and had been a Christian for fourteen years. She reported that this was the first time this had happened. Otherwise there were no other manifestations. Further counseling revealed some deep resentment towards her parents, and heavy occult involvement in the family before they all had become Christians. She also seemed to have a very weak will that was unable to stand up against the overbearing demands of her mother and boss at work.

It took the team three extended sessions to get her free from the demons. What we thought was the final battle took place on one of Archer Torrey's visits from Korea. He first asked her to make a list of all those whom she needed to forgive as well as any sins that she committed. These were confessed. In the midst of casting out evil spirits, Archer told her too that she had to resist the spirits herself.

This began a terrible struggle of her will against theirs. From our perspective, it seemed almost as if she was being attacked from outside. Throughout this battle there was a strange manifestation. Her arm involuntarily kept making frantic gestures of resistance. It looked as if she was repulsing some invisible attacker. After she fought off the spirits for a time, she seemed to be free. After this session was completed, I saw her at the hospital where she worked as a nurse. She looked very happy and told me that there had been no more trouble. The deliverance, however, was not complete.

A year and four months later she attended another prayer meeting in a large Presbyterian Church. At this meeting she came to me and another co-worker named Grace Low and asked for prayer. She said that a few nights before, she had felt a strange dark power enter into her body. It had settled in her right breast which from that moment had begun to hurt.

Recalling what had happened the first time I prayed for her, I was reluctant to start the prayer without the team. But they were all tied up in another exorcism. So we went ahead. I asked my coworker Grace to place her hand on the girl's breast. Then we prayed for her. As we did she went into violent spasms which threw her down on the floor. As before, her right arm started moving autonomously with actions of intense resistance. After settling her down, we asked why her arm kept doing these things; she said she did not know and looked very frightened. I bound the spirits and commanded them not to hurt anyone. Then in the name of Jesus I ordered them to leave her arm and breast and be bound together in her stomach. Then I commanded them to come out. This they did with violent struggle, intense gagging, retching, and large amounts of mucus. She seemed endowed with supernatural strength; it was all we could do to restrain her. Twice we were thrown to the floor.

We were soon joined by the rest of the team and went through this procedure three or four times. Each time, even though we commanded the evil spirits not to call in reinforcements, they seemed to come back more intensely than ever. Each time we prayed for discernment as to their ground of entry, but could get nowhere. This went on for about an hour. It was late and we were all exhausted. We felt that despite the clear evidence that spirits had been cast out, we had not touched the controlling spirit that was within her. We kept probing with questions, and kept commanding the spirit to tell us its name and ground of entry. During all this we had the girl's full active cooperation, but all to no avail. We were all completely baffled as to how to break through.

We were ready to leave, but Ken Shay, who had the strenuous task of preventing her from hurting herself or us, kept saying, "There are some big ones left in there, but how do we get to it?" Finally, we just stopped everything and asked the Holy Spirit again to come and reveal the source of the problem. As we waited, suddenly a strange image entered my mind—a fetus happily at rest in its mother's womb. Suddenly this peace was disturbed by a long tube-like object pounding against the womb and then the child. The child was being attacked and wanted to flee but could not. I was embarrassed to speak out what was in my mind, fearing that it was just my imagination. Finally, after seeking guidance, I shared the vision and asked the woman whether there was any trauma before birth. Had her mother attempted an abortion or something like that? She did not know, but said that her mother was right out in the hallway waiting, we could just ask her.

When we first told the mother the vision she did not have any idea what it meant, and then suddenly she began to cry. She told us that while pregnant with this daughter she had been seduced and raped. This was apparently the root of the strange resistance, as well as the entry for the demons.

I then led in prayers for emotional healing. We asked the Holy Spirit to lead us and to heal the brokenness resulting from this prenatal experience. At the strong prompting of the Holy Spirit, I then described again the vision. As I did the woman seemed to relive the whole terrible experience. Afterwards we asked Jesus to enter into the situation and to heal it for her. Another vision came of the fetus being bathed in light and held in God's love. Other team members were aware of the light that seemed to be shining upon her. One could sense that some deep healing was taking place. After a while she was able to forgive the man who had done this to her and to her mother. She was also able to forgive her mother. When this forgiveness was completed, and words of absolution were spoken over her, a look of wholeness and peace came upon her face. We all took a break and let her rest.

The team then regathered, laid hands upon her and prayed quietly in tongues or offered words of praise to Jesus. I then, while looking into her eyes, commanded any spirits that may have entered through this man, the experience, or through the unforgiveness of the mother, to come out. Immediately the woman was thrown on the floor, violently retching, and choked up a great deal of white mucus. Then it was gone.

We were all overcome by a sense of wonder at the obvious love and power of Jesus Christ. We then had an extended time of praise and celebration. Afterwards, the daughter and her mother went around warmly thanking everyone for their prayers. It was beautiful to see God work like this. We left exhilarated and exhausted.

This beautiful child of God is now delivered from the torment of evil spirits and is growing in emotional wholeness as well as in faith in Jesus Christ.

Summary of this type

Most of the deliverance ministry that I did in Taiwan was of this type and similar to these three cases. The inner hurt and misery was heart-breaking. It is clear that the Devil does not play fair; he picks on those who, often through circumstances beyond their control, have been made weak and defenseless.

It seems that the damage done by the demons is limited to that person and to their immediate family or friends. Besides the destruction of the individual's soul and the hindrance of the Kingdom of God, the demonization seems to serve no grander purpose. It has more the character of a bully or a vandal that wantonly destroys than that of a military commander with clear objectives.

This type of deliverance work is an expression of God's love and mercy. It is also an expression of the coming of the Kingdom of God, causing the downfall of Satan, and bringing wholeness and healing to those whom he has oppressed. For those who observe this type of ministry, it is a witness to the reality of demons as well as to the reality of the power and love of Jesus Christ.

8

TYPE FOUR: A STAGING AREA TO ATTACK A CHURCH, MINISTRY OR NATION

In the cases previously given, the sphere of the evil spirit's influence has been limited to tormenting individuals and their families. My reading of *Blumhardt's Battle* and other such literature suggests that there are more ominous possibilities. Blumhardt's experience of a woman who had become an entryway into our natural realm for large numbers of demons seemed so extreme that I discounted it. But then I started encountering cases in which the spirit's designs and effects went far beyond the individual. This fourth type I find horrible to contemplate; indeed, I resisted coming to the conclusion toward which the evidence pointed.

This is the case where the person has become a staging area for demonic attack upon a whole church or ministry. The obvious danger here is to suggest that the person himself or herself is wicked or destructive, but this is not necessarily the case. Rather, the person is more the victim of the demons who use them as their invasion route. Healing here represents not only freedom for the individual, but also a spiritual victory of strategic significance to the advancement of the Kingdom of God.

In the cases that I have dealt with, there have been deep emotional hurts as well as heavy occult involvement. The deliverance itself may be a protracted struggle in which many different spirits, or groups of spirits, are dealt with. In each case the final engagement has, however, been with high order controlling spirits that have direct orders from Satan or other beings high in the Satanic hierarchy. These orders have to do with the targeted work of God's Kingdom such as a church or ministry.

As with the complex types, there is for this type much need for emotional healing and sometimes psychotherapy. The deliverance itself, however, is a battle of even greater magnitude and intensity than the other types. This type seems to represent a high level spiritual conflict taking place between the Kingdom of God and Satan for control of a piece of earth. The staging area and the battlefield is this person.

I am not suggesting a dualistic view of reality. Ultimately there is no contest. Christ is victor; but here on earth the struggle is very real. There may be real victories and defeats. In this sense, there is a transitional dualism but not an ontological dualism.

This type requires a team, and often extensive prayer support. The battles have been long and violent, not only requiring gifts of the Holy Spirit, but also men with very strong arms to restrain the person to prevent them from hurting themselves or those ministering.

I turn now to tell the stories of two extraordinarily courageous women who, through deep childhood hurt and occult involvement, were not only demonized themselves, but became unwilling "channels" of demonic attack upon others.

1. Charity Chen was the first encounter with this type of spirit

Charity was one of Laura's best English students at the Presbyterian Bible College. After graduation she became our first co-worker at the Lay Training Center, and played a key role in the difficult but exciting days of getting the ministry started.

At the age of one she had polio and was left crippled in one leg. Growing up with a crippled leg and being a girl in a family that wanted a son had left many deep emotional scars. On trips to Jesus Abbey in Korea and during a healing workshop in America, she went through intensive emotional healing. She had a radiant spirit, a gift of compassion, and effectively moved in the gifts of the Holy Spirit. But there was something that disturbed me. First, her past still was not healed; it tormented her. Second, was a check in my spirit that an undefined something was amiss. For instance, when in healing ministry together, we would often find that she was the one who ended up being ministered to. This was a subtle, but consistent distraction.

During the Tom White seminar, which I have already mentioned as the time when I started to move into deliverance ministry, the evil spirit that I had only vaguely discerned in my spirit was forced to manifest. As Tom was teaching on the practical steps in deliverance ministry, Charity became visibly agitated. Laura had mentioned to me in passing before the seminar had started, "Doesn't Charity look strange today, she is so dressed up and pretty, but there is something that does not seem right about her."

After the teaching session was over, several of us proceeded to minister to her. In a very short time we were engaged in a fierce struggle with several very strong evil spirits. When questioned, it turned out that as a small child her mother had offered her up to one of the idols in a Buddhist temple. A spirit had entered in at that time. The deep inner hurts of rejection and unforgiveness had also given other spirits the opportunity to enter.

As the deliverance proceeded with Tom White in the lead and me translating, we commanded the Spirit to give us its name. Several did and were quickly dealt with. As Tom continued in prayer and probing commands, suddenly Charity cast off the six men who were restraining her, and a powerful arrogant spirit rose up, not Charity. Charity's face and voice changed to one of total defiance. "I am the King of Darkness" the spirit said in English. The transformation that took place before our eyes was terrifying! This was something that had preyed upon Charity's hurts, but was not her—it was alien to the human spirit and from another dimension.

It told us that the girl belonged to it, not to Jesus. We asked how it had gotten in, and with obvious pride it told us. As the questioning proceeded, I became aware of a new and frightening dimension of spiritual warfare emerging. Tom commanded it to tell us what its orders were. Again with obvious pride and defiance it said, "We are to destroy Brad Long, to subvert the spiritual renewal work of the Lay Training Center, and derail the renewal movement in the Presbyterian Church."

A tremor of horror went through me as the demon revealed its purpose. And many things fell into place. Over the last six years the ministry on several occasions had nearly been destroyed. With each advance came subtle (and not so subtle) assaults against us as individuals and as an institution. These had come in the form of misunderstandings and breakdowns in personal relationships. There had been temptations to moral compromise or to abuse spiritual authority. We had also endured deep irrational discouragement, fear, and anger. In looking back, I could see that something had indeed been working relentlessly against us. At the same time, I could not but give thanks for God's overflowing grace and protection that never let us down.

After a struggle of several hours, three major spirits were cast out. The first came with violent shrieking and retching. Others, apparently greatly weakened, came out more quietly.

Charity, through whom these evil spirits had found their foothold, was innocent of any sinister designs or actions. She confided that since she became a Christian there seemed to be some presence or power warring within her. Only with great faith and persistence had she become a very useful servant of Christ. She has gone through a recovery process and has continued to experience deep inner healing. She has now finished seminary and is in very effective Christian ministry. She has special gifts of mercy, teaching and healing. God's grace has prevailed and overcome.

2. The girl with a legion of spirits and hurts

The church in which we encountered this case is a large dynamic charismatic church with effective evangelistic outreach. It is not surprising to find that it had been targeted for a special attack.

At a large evening meeting, while leading in prayers for the infilling and gifts of the Holy Spirit, one of the women started to act strangely. When I prayed for her, she was thrown on the floor and began to writhe in pain. The deliverance that followed was terrifying. It took three weekly sessions each lasting two to three hours to get her free. The demons were cast out, but there remained much need for emotional healing.

She was born before her mother was married. Then as a little girl, she had been abandoned by her mother, and nearly killed by her father. She has the vivid image of her father, who was either possessed or insane (or both), smashing her younger brother's head against the wall until his blood painted the wall red. When they laid him in bed, the bed was soon soaked with blood. Through intervention of neighbors the boy lived. Another time the father tried to kill her with a butcher knife, but she managed to escape. The father also lived a wild life with lots of women who were always in the house, drinking and gambling.

The occult connection was clear. When eight years old, during a time of desperation, she offered herself to an idol in a temple. In addition, her father had traveled to some of the famous temples in Taiwan with well-known powerful gods. He had offered this daughter and the other children to these spirits. This means going through a ceremony in which the soul is given to the god. The person's name is then carved in the large prayer wheel that always stands before the idol. Like everything in the temple, this "service" required a large donation. (I am not sure whether he did this by way of seeking good luck for himself or for the children or both.)

Through circumstances that I am unfamiliar with, she had become a Christian and a member of this Charismatic church for seven years. Her symptoms of oppression were as follows: She lived constantly with depression and a sense of being surrounded by a dark cloud. She also heard inner voices urging her to kill herself or saying that she did not belong to Jesus but to them. She had actually attempted to kill herself on several occasions. She also had an intense hatred of her father.

During the first deliverance session and the discussion that followed, Don (our pastoral counselor) saw clear signs of schizophrenia. But during the course of the deliverance, he changed his mind and decided that there was deep emotional hurt but no mental illness. Indeed, we were all amazed at the women's strength of will and essential wholeness and integrity of personality in the face of such overwhelming odds. It took remarkable courage for her to face the pain of her past and the darkness that was within her.

A book could be written on the struggle that took place. It was very complex. We dealt first with spirits related to her own hurts such as anger. We also dealt with spirits that had entered into her through her mother. The most significant of these was a mocking, laughing spirit. In a strange high-pitched voice, it keep mocking us and the girl. We found that it had entered because of the mother's trauma of being pregnant with no husband. Every time she had gone outside the house, the people in the village had mocked her. When we commanded it to leave, the girl laughed wildly and uncontrollably for a few minutes, and then it was gone.

These were easy to deal with and left with little resistance. Then as emotional healing began to take place, we moved deeper and deeper into her past and, lastly, into the occult involvement. The closer we got to the occult and to things related to her father, the more intense the resistance became.

Finally, after several weeks of prayer and ministry, we seemed to be dealing with very powerful demonic beings. We knew this for several reasons. First, the physical resistance was almost more then we could handle. It took Ken, who is very strong, and several others using all their strength to keep her from hurting me and herself. Second, on several occasions, an alien entity seemed to seize control of her whole body. When this happened there would come into the eyes and face an expression of evil arrogance that was both revolting and terrifying. Third, we also had inward images of the nature of the entities that we were dealing with. For me these came as a sense of swirling darkness like a black hole annihilating life. Others saw snakes, demonic faces, and other such symbols of evil.

In this case, the personality shifts were so obvious and the abuse so extreme that we thought it was very possible that some type of disassociation had taken place. We discussed at length the possibility that we were dealing with a multiple personality disorder. How could we know that we were really dealing with evil spirits instead of alternate personalities? This was vitally important for the approach to healing is different for each case. Demons must be cast out, but "alters" need to be integrated. This question troubled me until recently when Amel Whitaker, a pastoral psychologist in San Francisco, introduced me to some helpful rules of discerning the difference between alternate personalities and evil spirits. These principles are based upon his own work with possession and MPD and the work of John Freison. Among other principles, they suggested that when dealing with alternate personalities, however nasty or hateful they may be, there is the awareness of being able to enter into a personal relationship with them. Alternate personalities may also enter into a relationship with Jesus. Whereas with demons, there is no possibility of a personal relationship and a total aversion to Jesus. Their observations confirmed that we were indeed dealing with demons.

Their ground of entry had been the fact that she had been offered up to the idols. So before we could make any progress, this connection had to be broken. The poor girl, even though in terrible pain and fear, cooperated fully. The inner voices kept threatening to kill her if she destroyed their ground of entry. Nonetheless, she confessed her sin and rejected the spirits. She also recommitted herself to Jesus Christ. After she did this, as a sign that she was in Christ, I anointed her with oil. As I did, she screamed in real pain. She said between sobs that the demons hated the oil and were in torment and in turn were tormenting her.

After the spirits had been greatly weakened, we commanded them to tell us what their mission was, if any. A vivid vision at once came to the girl of a golden city with its foundations being dug out by black termites. She then said that their purpose was of undermining and destroying this charismatic church. We sensed that she was a channel and a staging area for a demonic host that was attacking this whole church. This was confirmed to be true by the church members present, and also by what we knew of the turmoil that had accompanied the church's growth in the power dimension of the Holy Spirit's work.

The turning point in the deliverance came when the women and others had a clear vision of a host of angels doing battle against the hordes of Satan. We could spiritually feel this battle raging, all the while the poor girl felt it in her own body; as in tremendous agony she writhed on the floor. There were several moments when we actually feared for her life, and for her own safety.

When this last battle was finished, she was delivered. Since then this brave girl has shown a dramatic and obvious improvement. The voices and other symptoms ceased and she is well on the way to emotional health.

Of all the cases, this battle was the most costly for me

personally. Being subjected to such blasts of irrational evil cast a cloud over everything I saw. I had to spend hours outside in the tangible realities of mountains and forest to push back this sense of darkness. During the three-week period that we were working to set this person free, my family and I also came under severe attack. I personally dealt with intense temptations and had a persistent sensation of a hideous demonic face mocking me. Just to keep my own balance, I had others praying for me. I also met nightly with a brother in Christ, Paul McLean, a Canadian missionary who served as my confessor, and most of all, as my friend.

Besides the encounters with the darkness, I was deeply affected by the misery and suffering of this person. I was appalled and felt a heartsick nausea in the pit of my stomach for her. I felt as Dante must have felt as he walked through the inferno and looked upon the sufferings inflicted upon the damned by demons.

All glory be to Jesus who through His cross has set us free from the torment of demons in this world and in the next!

The personal attacks against me lessened in their intensity after the last battle was won. I emerged with an unsettling awareness of the reality of hell, but also with an even deeper faith in the saving power and overcoming love of Jesus Christ.

Unfortunately, this story does not have a completely happy ending. The girl was delivered and was set on the way to psychological wholeness. But because of the great damage caused by her in the church and the intensity of the deliverance, the congregation rejected her. She has had to find fellowship elsewhere. This has hindered her complete healing, and has also robbed the church of the full benefits of this great victory in Christ.

Summary: Very costly but important work

These cases of strategic deliverance have been a very costly and time-consuming business, but they are essential to the advancement of the Kingdom of God. In the case of Charity, the work of renewal in the Presbyterian Church continues to flourish, and Charity has been redeemed for vibrant Christian service. In the latter case, the Holy Spirit overthrew a stronghold of Satan that was threatening to cripple a strategic Charismatic church. He also brought healing and deliverance to a child of God who had been in bondage to Satan.

9

TYPE 5: STRATEGIC SPIRITUAL WARFARE FOR KINGDOM ADVANCE

In the first four types of demonic experience, the spirits are engaged with persons. Their presence and work seem intermingled with the person's personality. As such, there is some degree of ambiguity between what the evil spirit is and what the person's psyche is. It is usually only in the manifest presence of the Holy Spirit and direct confrontational prayer that they come out of the woodwork, and manifest themselves to be separate alien beings.

I must here account for another whole genre of encounters

that are not directly connected to individual persons. Rather, these represent strategic engagements with the "strong man" who presides over a particular area, and blocks the advancement of the Kingdom of God. This type of encounter is suggested in type four in which we found that a person had become a staging area, or open door for demonic attack upon a church or ministry. But here we go beyond the involvement with a particular person to engage the high echelon controlling spirits directly.

This type of high level spiritual warfare is like the preparations before a military invasion. Before sending in troops to secure a beachhead, enemy supply lines must be cut, strategic command centers knocked out, and major fortifications destroyed. On the mission field, this type of warfare was often necessary before mission work could go forward.

The following are three examples of this type of high-level work:

1. Spiritual warfare at the Bible College before the Lay Training Center could be founded

In 1980 we were called to Taiwan as PC(USA) missionaries. Our official assignment was to the Presbyterian Bible College. We also knew that we were to somehow be the means of bringing renewal in the Holy Spirit to Presbyterian Churches in Taiwan.

The more we got to know about the Bible College, however, the more we wondered why God had called us there. It was an institution that was obviously about to die. During the previous twelve years, vision and direction had been lost. Changes in the church and society had raised many questions of whether the college was even needed.

The buildings and grounds had the look of neglect and decay. The student body was down to sixty and losing members. The faculty was laced with contention and infighting. The prevailing opinion of the church and many missionaries was that the school should just be closed, and the land and buildings sold.

Upon getting to know the realities of the situation, Laura and I really wrestled with God in prayer as to whether the school had a future and whether we were to be part of that future. The clear word from the Lord was that we were called to the college and were given a two-fold mission: 1) Putting the school back on a productive course, and 2) building a Lay Training Center.

When we moved to the Bible College in the summer of 1982, I had no idea where to begin to work for renewal. Except for Principal Wang, there was no real support. I had an excellent co-worker named Timothy Huang; but he, at this time, was not especially open to the things of the Spirit.

Most discouraging of all was the fact that the "atmosphere" of the land and school clearly worked against any renewal in the Spirit. There seemed a coldness, if not hostility, in the very atmosphere. It was strange, even on a beautiful day with a clear blue sky and blooming azaleas, one had to fight depression. These feelings did not come out of our own subjectivity. Many people, both missionaries and Taiwanese, experienced the same thing. One Taiwanese pastor told us that the one hour a week he taught there was the most difficult time of his week; he always left with a feeling of deep oppression. Obviously this type of milieu did not lend itself to building up the student body, nor to offering a place for retreats and conferences for spiritual renewal.

We sensed some spiritual force was at work, but it eluded our clear definition. Except to pray, we were at a total loss as to what to do. It seemed that the vision of renewal was impossible, and we were to have the dubious honor of presiding over the final demise of the college.

The breakthrough came in September 1982, when I attended a Charismatic Prayer Retreat in Jia Yi (in the Southern part of Taiwan about 100 miles South of Hsinchu) for Western missionaries. While people were praying for me, David Clotfelter, a friend familiar with the Bible College, had a vision of our house. In our house there was peace, but around the house there were swirling currents of black, dirty water. This vision initiated an extraordinary venture into the supernatural in which we engaged in an extended period of spiritual warfare against the demonic powers that were afflicting the Bible College.

During this prayer time, many strange things occurred. First, we were all aware that we were participating in a struggle that transcended time and space. There was the sense of invisible forces clashing just beyond the reach of our consciousness. Our role in this was in openness to the Holy Spirit speaking out the names of the spirits as they were revealed to us. For instance, at one point, a man from New Zealand who had no knowledge of the school suddenly declared, "Old bones!" "Old bones!" Everyone asked what the meaning of this was. I said I did not know. But we prayed anyway that the land would be cleansed. We thought that perhaps there had been tombs, or that offerings had been made to idols.

We knew that a battle had been won when two people saw clear visions. The first was of Jesus striding through the campus with a whip driving out a host of demons. The second was of the fire of the Holy Spirit falling upon our house, and from our house spreading to the rest of the campus. During this prayer time we all clearly felt that we had entered into supernatural conflict, but we had no idea what really had happened.

A few days later one of the members of the prayer group, a man profoundly sensitive to spiritual realities, walked with me around the entire property praying over it and claiming it for the Lord. On this prayer walk he would suddenly stop and say, "Yes, here! There is something here!" We would then pray that the spot would be cleansed by Christ's blood. Once again I was unsure what was accomplished by this. Actually, I was rather skeptical and somewhat embarrassed, and during the walk kept looking back to make sure no one was watching us.

My skepticism, however, did not last long. Several things happened as evidence that the effects of the prayer time had been real. The first was a clear change in the atmosphere—the heaviness and coldness had lifted. This was noted by others who knew nothing of these prayers. Students who lived in non-Christian homes said that walking onto the Bible College land was like stepping into a sanctuary away from the demonic. The second thing was that a little research concerning the history of the land showed that the word about old bones was right. The campus had been the site for a Buddhist crematorium and many old graves. Old bones were indeed there! The Chinese knew the land was haunted. That is the reason they were willing to sell it to the foreign missionaries. The places where my friend had sensed some lingering evil presences proved to be the locations of the crematorium and of several old graves.

This did not end the spiritual warfare, nor was it a "quick fix" to solve all the school's problems. We were surrounded by temples whose influence needed to be constantly resisted. We had to remain vigilant to attacks, especially as the Lord increased our effectiveness in power ministry.

Now, in looking back at this spiritual warfare in which high level spirits were dealt with and the land cleansed, we see that it marked a profound turning point in being able to move into a renewal ministry. This was the basic ground work, the establishing of a base, that made the turnaround of the school and the founding of the Lay Training Center possible. Over the next six years the school became the venue for a series of conferences and retreats in which many pastors and lay people were equipped for ministry in the gifts and power of the Holy Spirit.

2. Spiritual battles in PRMI's Oklahoma City office, not just in Taiwan

Please allow me a quick departure from Taiwan! This type of strategic spiritual warfare that precedes effective ministry is not just limited to the mission field, it is also in the United States.

When I was appointed Executive Director of Presbyterian and Reformed Renewal Ministries International in 1990, I stepped into a battle field! There are many dimensions to the spiritual warfare that we have had to wage. There is no need to go into the long and dreary history of conflicts and misunderstandings within the church over charismatic renewal. But, it is obvious that an alliance of human sin with the demonic have conspired to keep Christians from growing in the full power and gifts of the Holy Spirit that Jesus intended for us.

In January 1990 when I began my responsibilities, the ministry was financially desperate. No money was coming in. One week in particular was extremely difficult. A donor had given us $10,000 with which to buy a new computer system. To honor their pledge, that money was put "off limits." I also felt that God was testing me to see if I would be faithful to those who gave. It was the beginning of the month when gifts usually come in, but that week only about $100 had arrived. We had bills to pay that totaled $4000! With each day that went by it seemed that something was cutting off our lifeline. A pall of despair and gloom settled over the office. I fought with the temptation to use the computer money, but by the grace of God decided that we would just sink before touching that which God had set apart for a special purpose. I, personally, was ready to quit, and wondered why I had ever left Taiwan!

Finally, at the end of the week on Friday, it got so bad that some of the office staff just went home early. Carter Blaisdell, Susan (the book-keeper) and I were left. With feelings of desperation I called them into my office and asked them to pray. Having no idea even how to pray, we bowed our heads and just waited in discouraged silence.

Then the Spirit started speaking through images. Susan said, "You know it is as if there some heavy cloak being placed over us and this office, choking the life out of us." Yes! It was as if we were being suffocated and that our lifeline was being cut off. That lifeline right then was not only money, but also hope and trust in God's provision.

We started doing what we should have done before things had gotten so desperate. We asked God to tell us what we were up against. That seems obvious, but part of being under attack is that the enemy employs a type of "electronic warfare" that muddles your thoughts and dims your vision.

Names such as a spirit of suffocating control come to mind, a spirit that would cut us off from breath and life. (All this was consistent with the history of the ministry as well as the Presbytery.) There were also spirits that were related to greed that has been at the heart of the "Sooner culture" and the oppression of the Indians by the early settlers.

We then started to pray in the name of Jesus that these spirits would be bound and driven away. As we did, something started brooding in the upper corner of the office. It felt heavy, oppressive and dark. The more we prayed against it the stronger it became until suddenly I felt a constricting feeling in my chest and found it hard to breath. Something invisible was choking me. One thought was a frantic, "My God help! Cast this thing out in the name of Jesus! The other thought was, "This is ridiculous! This is just job stress." But then, Susan started choking as well, and Carter looked as though he was about to sink into a black hole. So I knew that this was not some subjective feeling on my part! As we continued to pray and commanded it to leave in the name of Jesus, the room cleared. I had a clear vision of a tunnel of light being made through a cloud of darkness.

Three days later gifts started coming in to meet our needs for that month!

Let us return now to Taiwan.

3. Being defeated while taking on the god of wealth

In the "turf battle" over the Bible College, we were called to deal with only a small piece of land. We cleansed the ground and drove out the spirits that had assignments against the school. We did not presume to take on the controlling spirits of the whole nation. Once, however, we got ahead of God's guidance and attempted to take on the "strong man" over the whole nation, and were driven back in defeat.

On this occasion about 90 missionaries from around the island gathered outside of Taipei at a mountain-top retreat center to pray for Taiwan.

It was Chinese New Year, which is an excellent time to have a retreat. Many of us had come partly to get away from the continuous noise of firecrackers. All the stores close; transportation comes to a halt. For the Chinese, it is time for the family and the veneration of the ancestors.

After some teaching on spiritual warfare, we decided one night to pray against the controlling spirits blocking the gospel in Taiwan. We asked the Holy Spirit to reveal to us who those spirits were. Immediately five people said the image of the Fa Tasi Shen had been strongly impressed upon them. This is, literally translated, "the God to make a fortune." Around Chinese New Year his image is everywhere, especially at the banks and places of business. With this image we believed that we had received all necessary guidance, so we plunged in and began to pray against this spirit in the name of Jesus.

We were rather loud as we proclaimed victory in Jesus. Some prayed in English, others in tongues. To make sure that the spirit understood us, some even prayed in Mandarin and Taiwanese.

In the midst of our enthusiastic prayers, nearly imperceptibly at first, but rapidly growing in strength, a malignant presence started to form in the middle of the room. Despite our urgent prayers and commands in the name of Jesus, the presence continued to grow until it filled the room and we were cowed into silence. It felt vicious, evil, and unclean. Clearly, we had forced a very powerful spirit to manifest.

We were really frightened! Our triumphant proclamations of Jesus's victory became urgent pleas for protection. As we backed off, so did it. In a few moments, as if waking from a bad dream, the presence was gone and the room returned to normal.

We were overwhelmed by the experience and adjourned the prayer meeting discouraged and puzzled. Why had we been unable to deal with this power in Jesus's name?

I suspect that we got ahead of God's guidance. We attempted this more as an exercise applying newly learned principles of spiritual warfare rather than out of clear calling from the Holy Spirit. There are also some other factors that contributed to our failure.

First, we took on the spirit at what must have been the height of its power. On that very night in thousands of households throughout Taiwan, this god was being worshiped. This served as a clear open invitation, as well as "legal grounds" for that spirit to have control over Taiwan.

Second, I suspect that we took on too much. Rather than picking a strategic area and building a strong base, we advanced too far, too fast. This was like attempting an invasion of a whole country without first securing a beachhead. We got ahead of God's timing. As smaller areas are taken for Christ, and more and more people give their hearts to Christ, then that Spirit will be progressively weakened until one day he will be cast down completely.

Third, there was brokenness in our own ranks. On the following night, the Lord gave one of the missionaries a vision of a basket with a hole in it. With the vision came the word, "You lack spiritual power because there are holes in your community." I am ashamed to say, but right then I was convicted of my own sin of holding a long-standing prejudice toward the Baptist and the Presbyterian churches in America. Before coming to Taiwan, I had served a small Presbyterian church in a Baptist area. I had been snubbed by the Baptist pastors who hinted that Presbyterians most likely were not saved. I also had a good store of contempt for the PCA for their legalism and rigidity. I really did not believe that either group could be open to the Holy Spirit. And yet, there at that retreat were some Baptist and PCA missionaries moving freely in the gifts of the Spirit. When I publicly confessed this, I found myself not alone in harboring such negative feelings toward different members of our group.

We had entered the warfare without adequate preparation.

4. Another shot at the same god, but this time with greater success

Another profound encounter with high level territorial spirits took place during a spiritual warfare workshop at the Lay Training Center in 1988.The Rev. Tom White of Front Line Ministries was the main teacher. After detailed teaching on how to go about this type of high level spiritual warfare, we decided to have a "lab" in which we would try out some of the principles. Despite warnings to the effect that this was not for the uninitiated, fifty or sixty people packed into the room.

To grasp the significance of what was about to happen, I must pause briefly to give some background. Taiwan, though a small island occupied by around 20 million people, is a racial hodgepodge. The islands' earliest inhabitants are the aboriginal people of Polynesian descent. They constitute 1% of the population and are formed into eleven tribes, each with its own language. They were pressed into the high mountains by migrations of Chinese from Fukin three hundred years ago who tended to settle along the coast. Today these Chinese descendants constitute about 70% of the population and are called Taiwanese. About the same time the Hakka people arrived and settled in the foothills. The name Hakka means "guest." For generations they have migrated through China to many parts of Asia. Though Chinese, they have their own distinctive language and culture. They are about 5% of the population. Then, in 1949 with the fall of the mainland to the communists, Chiang Kai-shek led a mass migration of people from Northern China. When the Nationalists first arrived in Taiwan, they brutally liquidated much of Taiwan's educated leadership, and imposed their own ideology, government and language upon the rest of the population. Mainlanders now constitute about 15% of the population. Long-standing political friction and racial discrimination exists between these different groups.

All these different racial and ethnic groups of Taiwan were represented in that one room that day. Tom led the session and I translated. As we waited upon the Lord for guidance someone suggested, "Well, why don't we just start with the big red fat guy up on top of the hill?" On the mountain, just above the Lay Training Center was a huge, red, eight-story tall idol depicting the

Chinese god of prosperity and wealth. This was a very active temple. On feast days tour buses from around Taiwan passed the Bible College gates on their way to burn incense to this famous idol.

This seemed a good choice, so we waited upon the Holy Spirit for further instructions. As we waited, words of knowledge started to flow—words of scripture, as well as vivid images revealing the nature of the beings we were aligned against. We started to pray that Jesus would break the power these spirits exercised over the people of Taiwan. As we prayed, a strange thing happened. We were led away from a focus upon the spirits and back to a concern for ourselves.

George Shu stood up and said that we needed to ask the Holy Spirit to reveal to us why the people of Taiwan were so vulnerable to this god of wealth in the first place. "Was it because of insecurity, was it because of the conflicts and hurts in our history?" he asked. As George spoke I could feel the Holy Spirit beginning to move in the group.

Suddenly, a Western woman married to a Taiwanese stood up and said that she needed to confess that she hated Taiwanese men because of the way that she had been treated. A tense silence followed and then the storm broke lose. A Taiwanese pastor trembling all over stood up and with tears streaming down his face said that he had always hated the Nationalists because of the many Taiwanese who had been killed when they first took over Taiwan. Then a Mandarin-speaking mainlander pastor stood up, also in tears, and asked forgiveness from his Taiwanese brothers for what his people had done. He also confessed his imperialistic pride and his dislike of Taiwan. A tribal pastor then followed, pouring out his hurt and anger at the rejection and prejudice that he had received from Taiwanese and Mainlander Christians.

In a few moments, the whole group were weeping and going to one another confessing ancient hatreds. I was so caught up in what was happening that I completely forgot to translate for Tom who was standing off to the side feeling like his carefully established principles of spiritual warfare had somehow gone astray.

Finally, after a long period of this confession, I stood and in Mandarin Chinese—the language common to all—gave words of absolution. Immediately, there was an eruption of praise and celebration. For a long time we passed the peace with hugs and tears of joy.

Then we were truly ready for spiritual warfare; for Satan, by our confession and reconciliation, no longer had a foothold within us.

It is true that the tour buses still take pilgrims to the god of wealth. But for those pastors, Jesus is victor. Across Taiwan the Kingdom of God advanced through many of these men and women who, with new freedom, returned to their churches to spread the fires of renewal.

Summary of the Strategic Warfare Dimension

This last type of spiritual warfare is something that I believe should be undertaken only at the sovereign leading of the Holy Spirit. God takes the initiative in this warfare, and we are invited to share in this work.

Strategic warfare is not to be done piecemeal, but as part of the overall cosmos-wide advancement of the Kingdom of God. The Commander-in-Chief of that operation is Jesus Christ.

I count it a great privilege that Christ allowed us to take part in this work.

10

DIFFERENT LEVELS OF DEMONIC BEINGS

In the first part of the Dunamis Project's manual for Spiritual Warfare[1], we deal systemically with the Biblical witness concerning the nature of evil spirits and the organization of the Kingdom of darkness. Please refer to that for a more theological, Biblical analysis of these spiritual realities.

The following is a listing of the various types of spirits that we

---

[1] Long, Brad,& Ken Shay & Tom White & Tom Willcox. *The Dunamis Project 5: Equipping for Spiritual Warfare and Kingdom Advance.* Black Mountain, NC: Presbyterian Reformed Ministries International (PRMI), 1999. pp. 42-80.

encountered in the course of the deliverance ministry in Taiwan.

1. SINGLE SPIRITS WHO DO NOT SEEM TO POSSESS MUCH POWER

These are generally the types met with in the cases of SIMPLE DEMONIC OPPRESSION. Often they give a single name that is related to their function such as "anger" or "lust."

2. COMPLEXES OF SMALLER DEMONIC BEINGS WHO COME OUT TOGETHER

Often no single name is revealed for these complexes, just the impression that there are a number of them bundled up together. In type THREE and type FOUR, we have many times encountered this phenomenon. They often come out either before or after dealing with more powerful spirits.

3. AUTONOMOUS PSYCHOLOGICAL COMPLEXES

In the midst of the deliverances there were occasions when it was clear that we were not dealing with demonic spirits at all, but rather with parts of the person's personality.

These were usually encountered in the form of powerful emotions surrounding some hurtful experience, a person, or a generalized class of people who had caused the hurt. Often, as has already been noted, evil spirits would be in some way connected to the complex, and would initially appear indistinguishable from it.

4. SOULS OF THE DEPARTED

Another genre of spiritual entities that felt and acted very differently from demons seemed to be the souls of the dead. Rather than engage in the inevitable debate whether these were actually the souls of the dead or demonic impersonations, I shall share just two experiences from the many that we had while in Taiwan.

One was what felt like the soul of a lost little girl who was lurking in our home on the campus of the Bible College. We had been away for a year on home assignment in the United States. We had just returned to our house that had been occupied by some students while we were gone. For the first month back, I kept having the fleeting awareness that there was a ghost in our house. I would catch movement out of the corner of my eye. And at night when I was working, something invisible would seem to try to get close to me. It was not a frightening experience at all, but rather it felt sad and lonely, as though whatever it was just wanted to be close. I really thought my mind was playing tricks on me as the result of jet lag or culture shock. Then one night as we were putting our six-year-old daughter to bed, we both felt this presence come into the room. I asked Laura if she had felt it and she said, "Yes, it feels like a lost little girl who is lonely and just looking for love."

That night we prayed for this spirit and commended it to Jesus. We even read the Bible story of Jesus welcoming the little children to come to him. We did this in English and in Chinese. We did not feel it again. We never did find out why it was there, but suspected that there was some deep sorrow involved.

Another instance took place at a revival meeting at a Presbyterian Church. A man who was a committed Christian asked for prayer for a strange condition. He had been walking along the road when right beside him a truck ran over a man on a motor cycle, killing him instantly.

At the same moment, this person seeking prayer felt the dead man's soul affix itself to him. It did not enter his thoughts nor seem to work within his mind. It had just hung around as an unwanted presence, like another person constantly shadowing him. This had persisted for several months and was very wearisome.

I had never heard of such a thing and just assumed that what had taken place was the transfer of a demon from the dead man to the living man, who was just at the moment of death walking by. So I took the approach of casting it out in the name of Jesus Christ. Nothing happened!

Finally, we all prayed and asked the Lord what to do. The guidance came, "Don't cast it out, but bring this lost soul to Jesus." So we did. We asked the soul if it wanted to have rest and peace. We told it that it was not allowed to stay on earth. Then we presented the Gospel of Jesus Christ. After this, the soul left and no longer clung to the person. That was a strange case!

There are many other experiences, but they all have to do with the situation of either ancestor worship or of the spirit medium contacting the souls of the dead, or even the spirit medium sending a soul to work mischief in someone's life. All of these cases could well have been evil spirits impersonating a soul in order to bring deeper bondage to ancestor worship or give the spirit medium power over others. However, in the two cases mentioned, they did seem to be actual souls of the deceased.

5. VERY POWERFUL SPIRITS WITH ORDERS FROM EVEN HIGHER SPIRITS

It seems clear that these have orders to destroy the person or a church. It is not clear to me whether they are actually spirits from very high up in the demonic hierarchy, or whether they have just gained their obvious power from having been allowed to stay in a person a very long time. Usually they seem surrounded by many smaller spirits.

Getting them out is a real battle. These are the types also found in type THREE and FOUR.

6. TERRITORIAL SPIRITS

Demonic beings that exercise authority over certain geographical territories. These were unattached to specific human beings and were dealt with directly, as in the cases of "Strategic Spiritual Warfare."

7. SATAN?

Once we dealt with a spirit that was incredibly strong. This one had a quality about it that was different from the others. We all felt that we were dealing with either Satan himself or some other spirit very close to the heart of darkness.

This was a complicated case in which there was much need for inner healing as well deliverance. Over a period of six months, this woman had made great progress and at times various spirits had been cast out. Finally, we got down to dealing with the controlling demon. After some preliminary prayer and counseling, the Holy Spirit gave the image of a large, gray snake coiled up inside of her.

When this was shared with the lady she said that it was strange, but from childhood she had always had the bizarre feeling that there was a snake-like presence within her. This vague awareness had persisted even after becoming a Christian and growing in leadership in her church. Further probing revealed that the ground of entry went back to the sad circumstances of her birth over fifty years before in Mainland China. Her father had been a wealthy playboy who had had many mistresses. Her mother was the unfortunate one who got pregnant. She married him, but left him before the baby was born.

During the four-hour battle that followed, many strange and revolting things happened. At one point, when we commanded the spirit to manifest, the woman actually seemed to take on the appearance of a large hideous snake. The eyes became dull, reptilian, the body with the arms to her side seemed elongated, and started weaving to and fro like a cobra ready to strike. There was something utterly alien and satanic about this thing that confronted us.

We bound it and commanded it to come out. As we did the woman started to gasp for breath, and then started to choke. Terror filled her eyes as she actually began to asphyxiate. In a flash of insight, that could only have come from the Holy Spirit, I shouted, "Open your mouth wide and pull the snake out." She caught hold of something invisible and started frantically pulling. As she did her mouth formed a rounded shape that grew larger and larger, until it looked as if her jaw would break. Suddenly, with one jerk, it came out. Even though she did not move from her chair, a tangible force, like the stench of death, struck me in the chest, throwing me against the wall. I was overcome by waves of revulsion, nausea, and weakness. The terrible thing, like pulsating energy which was clearly apprehended by the spirit, and dimly perceived by the natural eyes, swirled around the room and struck the woman, knocking her off her chair. As a protective reflex, we joined hands and prayed loudly in the Spirit, calling upon the name of Jesus. If we had not, there is little doubt that the thing would have reentered the woman.

This was followed by the expulsion of two other smaller snake-like entities. And then she was free.

We have met other, very high-level spirits on several occasions. In the above case of the snakes, no name was given. In other cases, they have variously identified themselves, as "The King of Darkness," or the name of some major Chinese deity. Demons are liars, but these powerful spirits, when revealing themselves, show such incredibly haughty arrogance about who they are that I suspect their pride has led them to tell the truth.

8. SPIRITUAL POLLUTION

Often after evil spirits have left, one has a sense of spiritual pollution or contamination. Experientially this may be a nauseating feeling of filth or uncleanliness similar to a violated conscience. The person needs to be cleansed. After a major deliverance, the team members often experienced this same need for cleansing.

We often did this by anointing with oil or washing with water. There is nothing magic about this. Rather the oil or water serve as vehicles for the actual presence of the Holy Spirit. Jesus used these visible vehicles in order to support our faith in Him.

To put all this in perspective, the following instance took place in the case of the person delivered of the snake-like spirit. After the spirits were cast out, we knew the person needed cleansing. But discovering that we had all forgotten to bring oil, I raced to the kitchen and poured out a rice bowl full of what I thought was cooking oil. After blessing it in the name of Jesus, I started to anoint the person's forehead and hands. As I did, one or two lingering demons manifested and were quickly dealt with. As we prayed, I noticed little bubbles and smelled lemons, and thought "that oil is behaving strangely." After everything was over and the person had obviously been set free, I discovered that the spiritual cleansing had indeed taken place with the best possible agent, soap detergent!

Along with the sacramental cleansing through anointing, there is also the need for human touch and acceptance. The delivered person desperately needs to know that even though something dreadful has been cast out, they themselves are accepted and loved. Often after a deliverance, there is much spontaneous embracing. This is a vitally important part of the healing process.

SUMMARY: WHAT ARE THESE THINGS?

These experiences that I have just related to you raise in me deep questions about the nature of reality and the nature of evil.

What are these things? Really? I know the traditional Biblical answer, "They are fallen angels." But that only leads to another equally perplexing question, "What are angels?"

We face a mystery. I do not know exactly what demons are or why they are allowed by a good God to exist. I do know from scripture and from these experiences that they are very real, and are the opposite of life, wholeness, goodness, and the light of God's Spirit. As to their ultimate nature, they are like parasites attaching themselves to human beings where they find a certain sympathy as well as nurture for their unholy existence. Yet they are not parts of ourselves; they are alien, non-human entities with a will and malevolent character of their own.

Zeb Bradford Long

11

JESUS CHRIST IS VICTOR

This ends my account of this phase of the encounters with evil spirits during this period of revival in Taiwan. At the rewriting of this booklet, as I am in the Blue Ridge Mountains of North Carolina amid the solid realities of streams, trees, and mountains, these experiences of the demonic have an unreal quality about them, like the fragments of nightmares.

God's love and creation seem so pervasive, the world rational and ordered, and yet I am haunted by what I know from experience to be real—we live in a fallen world in which there is evil, sin, and death.

In these encounters with demons, I found experientially that Paul speaks the truth when in Ephesians he writes:

"For we are not contending against flesh and blood, but against the principalities, against the powers, against the world rulers of this present darkness, against the spiritual hosts of wickedness in the heavenly places." (Ephesians 6:12)

In meeting first-hand these realities of which Paul speaks, I must affirm what the scriptures and the saints of every age have already revealed: The call to follow Jesus Christ is to receive life abundant. It is also the call to join the Lamb's war which is of vast dimensions and of ultimate consequence.

While meeting the reality of darkness, there were two greater realities that were touched in these experiences. The first was the strength and goodness of human beings. Just as war or some catastrophe may show what we are made of, so spiritual warfare reveals the tenure of our own human spirit. These spiritual battles have provided the occasions to look deeply into the powers of hell. And they are horrible. But at the same time there have been opportunities to see the human spirit, in Promethean dimensions struggling to be free and to restore itself to its only true nature of being in the image of God and free for God. I came to know heroes, for whom there will be no ticker tape parades, but who will surely receive honor at the great feast of the Lamb.

The second reality, but the most important of all, can only be expressed in words of praise and thanksgiving! This was experiencing the reality, the everlasting love, and cosmic power of Jesus Christ. Through the cross, Jesus of Nazareth, our resurrected Lord and Savior, is the Victor!

Unto the Father, and unto the Son, and unto the Holy Spirit, be ascribed in the Church all honor and glory, might, majesty, dominion, and blessing now, henceforth, and forever. Amen!

Made in the USA
Middletown, DE
19 January 2018